Simply Wrapped®

The Gift on the Outside®

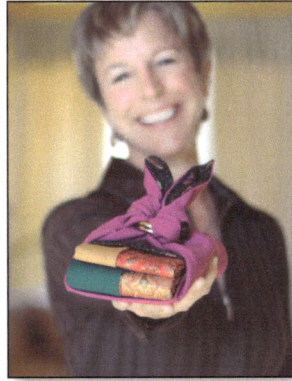

A Story

A Tradition

A Gift

Laurel Boone Helm

Roberts & Ross Publishing
COLORADO • FLORIDA • USA

Simply Wrapped®

The Gift on the Outside®

A Story, A Tradition, A Gift
by Laurel Boone Helm

ISBN: 978-0-9822015-0-3 *(paperback)*
First Edition

PUBLISHER Roberts & Ross Publishing
ENGLEWOOD, CO
(303) 762-1469
SANTA ROSA BEACH, FL
(850) 622-5772
RobertsRossPublishing.com

SENIOR EDITOR Max Regan

ART DIRECTOR Sheila J. Hentges

BOOK DESIGNER & PRODUCER COVERS & INTERIOR
Sheila J. Hentges

PHOTOGRAPHERS COVER & STORY
Peggy Dyer Photography

STEP-BY-STEP INSTRUCTIONS
Deb Mizell

ILLUSTRATORS STORY
Alison Magovern

STEP-BY-STEP INSTRUCTIONS
Sheila J. Hentges

To Dad

Acknowledgements

Tis a simple matter to wrap a present,
not so to make a business out of an idea
and then to write a book.

■

I'D LIKE TO THANK my husband Roger for creating the Simply Wrapped work place I needed, and then creating it again, and then again, and then again each time we moved. To my son, Colby, who has *always* believed in Simply Wrapped and in me. And to my son Justin who would not even think to wrap his gifts in anything other than Simply Wrapped cloth wraps. To my sister Susie whose wisdom and love has buoyed me up on countless occasions. And to my sister Carol who has the energy of an army of women and would never let me sit long enough in a blue state to have one doubtful thought. Work!! You will feel better!

To Tricia for always being there to listen, brainstorm, and problem solve when this whole business of business got overwhelming. And to her family, Bill, Sam, and Luke for being my first family of converts.

To Linda Lenox you are such an inspiration!

To my Chief Elf, Deb. Thank you for being so dedicated to the cause and for the countless hours of unscheduled photo sessions when I needed yet "one more photo."

To Peggy Dyer, what an eye you have! Thank you for seeing what others don't and being able to capture it in your magic lens.

To my editor Max Regan for doing an amazing job coaching the story out of me. To Shireen Day for being my first reader and usability tester.

To Alison for all your wonderful enthusiasm and willingness to step into unknown territory—you're terrific!

To Patricia Ross and Sheila Hentges for being the team I needed.

And to all the local sewers who sewed the hundreds of wraps in the eleventh hour. Thank you all. May your gifts be enhanced by the fabric that wraps them.

Contents

The Story of
Simply Wrapped

WHEN I WAS SIX YEARS OLD, my dad bought a huge
amount of Christmas paper—rolls and rolls of the same print.
I'm sure that he got a good deal on it. There were seven of us,
and my dad was raising us on his own. We needed to watch our
pennies back then, and so Dad, bless his heart, used that paper
to wrap *all* of our presents. What I didn't know for many years
was that he also used the same paper on each of our presents
so that no one felt more "special" in any given year than the
other kids. We were all loved equally by my dad, and this was
yet another way that he showed us. For years, when we woke
up on Christmas, there under the tree were presents for all of
us, each wrapped in the same big-eyed reindeer paper.

It was Christmas 1993. I had my own family, and I sat on the
floor after our traditional opening of presents, stuffing the
piles of torn wrapping paper from our family of four into huge
black garbage bags. One of the wrapping paper prints, a green
background with big eyed reindeer, reminded me of my father.

As I stuffed the crumpled paper into the trash bag that Christmas morning, I realized that I wanted that reindeer print back. I wanted something that would remind me of my brothers and sisters, the holidays, special occasions and the joyous times I had experienced as a child. I didn't want all this paper trash. I didn't want the waste and the lost memories. I wanted our gifts, the gifts given from then on, to be given with more thought, more heart.

I didn't sleep very well that night or for several nights afterward. I imagined folding fabric around gifts, creating something with the wrapping that was amazing, unforgettable, flexible, easy to work with, forgiving. There were lots of paper and fabric bags on the market, but bags are confining, a bag, after all, can only ever be a bag.

"Roger, I need to go to the fabric store," I said to my husband as we sat over coffee a few weeks after the holidays.

"Well that's new," he said. "What do you need at a fabric store?"

"Fabric. Honey I have this great idea for a product that I really think will enhance the experience of giving. Not only will it support the environment, but it could be a part of family tradition. I really think it will sell."

"Hmm" he said, looking skeptical.

"Wouldn't it be great if we never bought another roll of wrapping paper to wrap our family gifts in, ever again?"

"Yes it would. The waste really bothers me."

"Exactly!"

"Are you thinking of wrapping in fabric?"

"Yes."

"But wouldn't that be expensive? Wouldn't it be difficult to wrap all the weird sized packages in fabric?"

"That's why I need to go to the fabric store. I don't know what fabric costs or exactly how it will work. I need to try it and see."

"Who would buy fabric gift wrapping?"

"Do you know how many gifts are wrapped every year for Christmas and Hanukkah? Then there are birthdays and other gift giving occasions. Honey, this will work." I said, flying high from the dream of it all.

"If you say so," he said one eye brow up as if to say *I'll believe it when I see it.*

"Oh, come on have a little faith." I said.

SEW MARKS

Later in the afternoon we went into the local fabric store with our two sons Colby, seven, and Justin, nine, in tow. It was just after Christmas so all the holiday prints were on sale and I started piling fabric into the cart.

"Honey, do you really need this much fabric?" Roger asked, clearly worried.

"I need to make a lot of these," I say, "and these prices are great."

Of course at the time I didn't consider that the reason the fabric was so cheap was that all the prints were out of date.

I pulled my basket up to the stand for the cashier to ring up. Roger's expression went from worry to despair as I pulled out my credit card and charged over five hundred dollars worth of fabric.

"Are you sure you know what you are doing?" he asked.

"No, but the only way to learn is to begin. It'll be okay, dear," I said. "I just have this feeling that I need to do this." This comment wasn't particularly comforting to Roger, and I understood. But I took the fabric home anyway and began to experiment.

The following weekend I dug the sewing machine out of the attic, set it up in the family room, and started up the learning curve.

"What's that, mom?" my son Colby asked me.

"It's a sewing machine," I told him

"How does it work?"

"I don't know," I said thumbing through the manual.

After much experimenting, I called my sister Carol, the sewing expert.

"I want to put two pieces of fabric together, and you know, make sew-mark things. It should be easy but I'm not sure where to start. Can you give me some pointers?" After waiting a respectable amount of time for her to stop laughing, I told her to please control herself and answer the question.

"First of all, they aren't called 'sew marks' they are called seams. And second, are you *really* attempting to sew?"

"Oh, stop it," I said. "I have this idea for a product that I want to try out and I need to sew to do it."

"Why don't you just send the fabric to me and tell me what you want?"

"That would be great!"

"What is it that you want?"

"Just two pieces of fabric sewn together"

"Okay, I need to know a little more than that."

"I'm not exactly sure how it is going to work, but the pieces should be square, I think."

"How big?" she asked

"Um, about a square yard."

"That's pretty big," my sister said.

"I'll know better after I've experimented a little."

"Well send the fabric to me and then call me when you know what you want."

"Thanks, Sis. You're great."

"And you're crazy," she added before saying goodbye.

I hung up the phone and sat wondering if she was right. What had happened to me? I had a great paying job at IBM as a writer, my family and I had a wonderful home in an equally wonderful neighborhood; so why did I feel so restless? And why did this simple idea of how to transform the art of gift-giving seem so important to me?

PRACTICING

Over the following weeks I experimented with wrapping things in fabric and I did some research, knowing that fabric wrapping was not a new concept. Asian cultures have been wrapping in fabric for literally thousands of years, but still I could find nothing specific on the internet or in libraries and bookstores, so I forged ahead with my own creative ideas.

I wanted to use cotton because of its durability and stiffness. I'd eliminated the idea of wrapping in a single layer of fabric for three reasons: first, you could see through the fabric; second one layer didn't have the stiffness I needed to create shape; and third, with two sides (one print one solid) I could use the same wrap for two totally different occasions. And I'd also decided, after much experimenting with different shapes, that a square was the right shape. It allowed the most versatility.

I sewed squares of fabric together and wrapped things with them, books, vases, boxes, weird shaped things and anything I thought could possibly be given as a gift. At first the wrapped gifts looked like a wad of fabric, shapeless and unattractive, not the beautiful images I'd imagined. So I had to adjust my thinking; after all, fabric has to be approached differently than paper. I needed to relax and enjoy the process of wrapping, and to work with the properties of fabric; soft, moldable, strong. I wrapped and rewrapped hundreds of items.

Sometimes I'd dream about shapes at night and have difficulty sleeping until I tried to create what I saw in my mind.

"Laurel, are you wrapping again?" Roger asked sitting up in bed at 1:00 a.m.

"I'm sorry dear, I just had this idea for a wrap and I wanted to try it out."

"Can't you do it in the morning?"

"I'm done. See, isn't it beautiful" I said, holding up the wrapped gift.

"What did you wrap?" he asked

"Your book."

"The one I'm reading?"

"Um, yeah…do you mind if I don't unwrap it right away? I need to make notes on how I did this."

Roger sighed. "I suppose. Will you turn off the light now?"

SETTING MY HEART

I found that during this stage of the creative process it was best not to share my ideas too often and to be very careful whom I shared them with when I did. This was not because of the threat that someone might steal my idea but because the continuous unsolicited advice I kept receiving made it hard to think clearly. In the beginning, when I'm creating something new no matter what it is, it is not just the end result that I'm after, it is the journey of getting there; that's what makes me feel most alive. That's not to say that I didn't listen to advice when I was ready; whenever I had a block or a gap in knowledge I'd seek the help of an expert.

The more I explored the idea of fabric wrapping the more I felt overwhelmed by the amount of work it would take to make my dream a reality. On a visit to Spokane, Washington where all my extended family lived, I shared my idea with my family, in the secret hope of enlisting some help.

 "We wouldn't use paper any more. And remember that reindeer paper?" I asked my two sisters and my dad, who were sitting at the kitchen table of the home we grew up in.

"The Reindeer paper. How could we forget that? We used that paper forever," My sister, Carol said.

"I got a good deal on that paper," Dad said defending his reasoning for buying mass quantities of the paper which had taken us years to use up.

"We loved that paper, Dad. I still have a small piece of it left." Susie said.

"Anyway, with this product, we could have that same print on fabric and have that print last forever," I told them.

"It's a good idea," Susie said.

"If we all worked together, I know we could make this into a great product."

There was an awkward silence as they all looked down. This was my first clue that there would be no *we* in this adventure. Their lives were too busy with their own families to take on starting a company with me. I understood and I didn't press it.

But we sat together in the bright kitchen, the four of us brainstorming on how the product would look. The more we talked the more depressed I felt. I had absolutely no idea how to turn an idea into a business and doing it all alone felt impossible.

That is when my Dad looked at me and said, "You can do anything you put your mind to."

Our parents say millions of words to us over our lifetime, most of which we tend to forget but some words we always remember. What dad said wasn't profound, it probably wasn't even the first time he had said it, but for some reason the look in his eyes, said something more. It was as if he was saying he now understood, there at the end of his life, the immensity of the human spirit. *You can do anything you set your heart to, believe, begin, and don't give up.*

I returned home from my trip understanding that if this idea was going to become anything real, then I'd be doing the work alone and I needed to be patient with myself. This was likely going to take a lot longer than I'd thought. If I had only known how long….

WHAT TO NAME "IT"

I spent months considering a name for my idea, but naming is a creative process that can't be rushed. One day when I was looking for a new book to read at the bookstore I ran across a novel called *Time and Again*. It's about a time in history when things were simple.

Simple....

Later I was sitting in a coffee shop and I heard a song that I'd never heard before. "Tis a gift to be simple, Tis a gift to be free..." the lyrics came over the speaker.

It is simple, a simple gift, a gift wrapped simply.

"Honey, I think I have the name for my product" I told Roger when I got home from the coffee shop.

"Really, that's great. What is it?"

"Simply Wrapped."

"I like it," he said as he opened the refrigerator, "What's for dinner?"

I'm always amazed how I can be consumed with an idea for a product while he is consumed with ideas of food. I guess they are related; both come from a kind of hunger.

It was such a relief to have a name for my idea. It felt a lot like when we had settled on names for our children. Until something is named it resides in a spiritual realm that only you as the creator can recognize. Once named, it is born.

LESSONS ON THE WAY

After finding a name for it, I started using Simply Wrapped gift wraps for every occasion. Now that it was really in the world, (my world anyway) I needed to feed it, to use it. The first time outside of Christmas I used my wrapping was at our son Colby's eighth birthday party.

"It's time for cake and presents, guys" I said as I called for the boys to come down from the family room where they were playing. The sound of several feet came bounding down the carpeted stairs onto the hardwood floors of the living room.

"Cake or presents first?" I asked Colby.

"Presents!"

"Okay then, this way" I said as I ushered the boys to the den where I'd put the presents on a small round table. One of the boys broke away from the group, went to the table and reaching out touched one of the presents.

"I like this one" he said. It was the gift from me to Colby. It was Simply Wrapped. The boy held the corner of the wrap between his fingers feeling the cloth and smiling.

Wow he gets it. I thought *Children are amazing, they see what adults often lose the ability to see.*

It was Christmas again, only this year there was no sound of scissors and paper and tape. Instead of feeling wasteful, I felt wonderful, as I wrapped everything in the fabric wraps I'd made earlier in the year. There is nothing quite so invigorating as seeing an idea come full circle.

"Mom, are those our presents?" Justin asked as he looked at the gifts on end of the table where I was wrapping.

"Yep. What do you think?"

"They're great."

"Where's the gift you got for Colby?" I asked him

"I hid it in my bedroom." He said

"Why don't you go get it and you can use this to wrap it." I said holding up a Santa print wrap.

"Okay," he said as he ran upstairs to retrieve the gift.

Wrapping in fabric was difficult at first for the boys but no more difficult than wrapping in paper.

"How's this mom?" Justin asked holding up the gift he'd wrapped.

"That looks very nice. You can put it under the tree if you want."

"I'm going to show Dad first."

I finished wrapping, taking my time to enjoy the process. It didn't take long and there was no mess to clean up. It seemed very natural.

On Christmas day after our traditional cinnamon rolls,
we went into the front room to open gifts.

"Look boys," Roger said standing in front of the Christmas tree,
"do you notice anything different?"

They both looked puzzled.

"The gifts are all wrapped in fabric."

"Oh yeah we saw that didn't we?" Justin asked, elbowing Colby.

"Yeah, that's right." Colby said nodding a little too vigorously.

"Who's passing out the gifts," Roger asked.

"Me!" said Justin

"Okay, you are the Passer."

Justin sat at the base of the tree and picked up the first gift.

"It doesn't say who it is for," he said turning the fabric
wrapped gift.

"Oops," I said, "I forgot to mark them!"

"Mom!"

"One small glitch in the process, huh dear?" Roger
said laughing.

"Let me see that gift," I said

Justin handed me the gift and I felt it.

"This one is for Colby."

"Maybe you need to be the Passer." Roger said smiling.

"Next year labels would be good, mom." Justin said laughing

We finished opening our gifts and one by one I folded up the wraps and placed them in a box for next year.

"This really is pretty neat." Roger said as he looked into the box of carefully folded fabric wraps. "Not a single piece of wrapping paper. Well, except the ones my parents sent."

"It sure feels better than last year." I said "No waste and nothing to clean up."

HOLDING PATTERNS

I had to put the idea of turning Simply Wrapped into a business on hold in 1995 while we moved our family across the country from North Carolina to Washington state to take over the family farm. Still, I could not give up the idea that others would like Simply Wrapped as much as we did in our family and that someday people would tire of the waste of wrapping gifts in paper. So even on the long drive across the states we experimented with Simply Wrapped. It was a way to help our boys pass the time and for me to keep my dream alive.

"Here guys, help me come up with additional ways of wrapping gifts with Simply Wrapped," I said as I handed both of the boys a pretend gift and a wrap.

"What are we supposed to do?" Justin said as he looked at the book and the wrap lying in his lap.

"Wrap the thing I gave you like it is a gift you are giving to someone you really like."

He continued staring at the wrap and book.

"Here I'll get you two started." I said laying the wrap out flat on the seat and showed the boys the first steps.

The boys continued quietly in their seats, wrapping.

"Look mom," Colby said from the front seat, showing me his wrapped jar of Salsa. (He had won the paper, rock, scissors challenge and so had gotten to ride shotgun.)

"That's great, Colby, it looks like a wizard" I said, and it did.

At ten, Justin wasn't too into the wrapping. I understood. Wrapping isn't for everyone but even for people who don't like to wrap gifts, Simply Wrapped can be so much easier than paper once the basics are mastered. But when he was finished he was satisfied with his efforts.

NEVER GIVING UP

My Simply Wrapped family collection had grown in the two years since its inception. It was Christmas 1995; we were settled into our temporary home, and I was preparing to celebrate the holiday with my brothers and sisters. I pulled out the cardboard box of wraps and looked through the colorful prints picking up and feeling the fabric. It was so soft and forgiving. I loved wrapping my gifts in them, knowing that the process would not only be fun but that the wrap would be reused. I knew that, for my family, the wraps I used for them would begin to contribute to the memories of the occasion. This was the first year I'd be able to wrap presents for my extended family. I sat at the dining room table. The presents (mostly cakes I had baked myself) and the wraps I'd chosen for each of my family members were laying around me in stacks.

"Want to help me wrap gifts?" I asked Roger, who was in the kitchen looking for something to eat.

"I think I'll leave the wrapping to you," he said, coming around the corner with an apple in his hand.

"Okay, but you're missing out on some fun."

"I'll just watch you; that's enough fun for me." He said.

I began with the small cakes I'd baked, wrapping and re-wrapping.

"I thought it was easy."

"Well it will be once I learn how to do it. Wrapping in Simply Wrapped is an art, not a science." I tell him.

"You should be writing an instruction book," he says.

And as I worked to find the best way to wrap the various sized gifts, I realized he was probably right.

I picked up my gift to my brother, two books I had found in my collection when I was unpacking. They had belonged to him as a child and were inscribed in his childish handwriting. I knew he would be very surprised and I wanted the wrap to be perfect. I chose a print with a black background, stars and angels in gold, with highlights in red and white. It was masculine, yet festive. I laid the fabric out, placed the books in the center and folded and knotted the fabric so it looked like a bow tie. When I presented it to my brother he looked at the gift turned it over and smiled, "This is great. Is this what you were talking about?"

"Yes," I said, "This is Simply Wrapped."

I looked at dad as he sat in his wheelchair. He was smiling as he watched the reactions of my siblings.

After opening presents we sat around and visited. I went into the kitchen to refill a plate of food. My brother followed me.

"Simply Wrapped is a great idea but will take time and money to develop."

"Yeah, that's the challenge…time and money," I said.

It already felt like an eternity since I'd conceived Simply Wrapped two years earlier. I was learning to be patient, knowing that this was my baby and I'd have to carry it forward, one step at a time, in between all the other things going on in the rest of my life.

My greatest supporter was always my dad. I'd visit him nearly every day in the care center were he lived. On one of my visits I took him a small gift of food, (he hated institutional food) wrapped in Simply Wrapped using the print called Hunter Gone Fishing. He would talk to me about Simply Wrapped and ask how it was going. I told him it was going slowly but that I worked on it when I had time and extra money.

"It's going to take more than we have to take the concept to the next level. I think I'll look into a bank loan." I explained.

"How much do you need?" he asked

"About $5,000.00 I think. I have a little more research to do before I know the right number to go to the bank with."

"I'll give you the money." he said.

I sat thinking about it for while. He nudged me with his arm, smiling encouragingly.

"Are you sure?" I asked. "I can't guarantee you'll get it back soon or at all, it's a risk."

"Yes," he said. "Take the money and make Simply Wrapped into a business."

My father died of colon cancer the following summer long before Simply Wrapped was launched, but his belief in me and in Simply Wrapped is one of the main reasons I've never given up.

INCH-BY-INCH

The ten years on the ranch in Cheney, Washington took all of our energy, between kids, my job and restoring the old farm house, there was very little room left over for my entrepreneurial endeavors. But with the funding dad had left me and some creative time management, I found time to keep Simply Wrapped inching forward, year after year and with each passing year Simply Wrapped became more and more a part of our lives.

"What are you doing?" Roger asked when he saw me in the living room still littered with pieces of trim and walls waiting for the next coat of paint. I'd placed one of the old windows we'd removed across the top of two saw horses and put a shade-less lamp on the floor beneath it. It was Fall of 1997 and we were fully engulfed in recreating the ranch and making a home.

"I'm making a light table so I can trace the pictures I took of the steps for wrapping. I'm creating an instruction booklet." I told him.

"Oh," he said looking over my shoulder. "Wouldn't it be easier to just draw them?"

"If I could draw, yes."

"I see. Ok. Don't forget we need to move the herd tomorrow," he said and went off to bed leaving me still consumed in Simply Wrapped.

I sighed, looking down at my sketches through the light, trying not to count the hours I had left to work and sleep before I would be up saddling my horse and up to my ears in cattle.

TRADITIONS TAKING HOLD

"Okay, Mom, close your eyes and hold out your hands," Justin said his eyes shining with excitement. It was my birthday.

"Don't look, Mom!" he said

"It's not something slimy is it?" I asked him. Justin was thirteen so the idea wasn't unthinkable.

"No Mom I promise."

"Okay" I said holding out my hands. I felt the fabric and opened my eyes.

"Wow look at this! It's great Justin."

"What do you mean, you haven't even opened it."

"The wrapping silly. You used Simply Wrapped"

"Well of course I did. What else would I use?"

He smiled, clearly proud of himself.

I opened it and honestly I don't remember the gift. What I remember is that he wrapped my present himself using Simply Wrapped and didn't seem to think twice about it.

One of the hardest things for people who have received a gift Simply Wrapped to do is to use it to wrap another gift and give that wrap away. I suppose it's this tendency we have to hold onto stuff. So when my sister wrapped my birthday gift that year in the wrap I'd given her the year before, I could really feel the tradition taking hold. It was 1998, and we'd been using Simply Wrapped for four years.

CHAIN SMOKERS, FISHING LINE, AND THIEVES

When I wasn't using the time I'd set aside for creating products for Simply Wrapped, I was learning about how to setup and run a business. Setting up the entity and getting a registered trademark was easy, but finding suppliers for the fabric and a manufacturer to sew the wraps was much harder.

I'd found a supplier, though the cost of the fabric was much higher than I had hoped to pay. I updated my business plan to include creating our own line of prints and working directly with the textile manufacturer, something for much further down the road.

Finding a good local manufacturer to have my first wraps sewn was a challenge, as nearly all the textile manufacturing had gone overseas.

I opened the metal door to the entrance to the warehouse where I planned to meet the manufacturer, a man in his early 40s who owned and operated the company. The warehouse was full of sewing machines, the type used for heavy industrial sewing like canvas. A couple of women were working on a heavy canvas tarp like the kind that might be used to cover a boat.

They looked up. "Can I help you?" One of them asked.

"Yes, I'm here to meet Tom Barker," I said.

"Up here," a man said from top of a flight of stairs that led to the offices on the second floor of the building. "I'll be with you in just a couple minutes."

I stood there waiting in my IBM dress suit and heels, feeling very out of place. The women working on the other side of the room looked me up and down. After what would have been an unacceptable length of time even by IBM standards, Tom finally asked me to come up to his office. I'd always treated potential customers with the greatest respect and consideration, but clearly these folks didn't follow the same protocol.

"Have a seat," he motioned to the wooden chair on the opposite side of his desk. His office was cluttered with stacks of papers, magazines, and miscellaneous product samples.

"What is it you need sewn?" He asked, looking down on me from his elevated chair.

"I just need to have two pieces of fabric sewn together. I brought samples."

"Good, let me see them."

I handed them to him. He glanced quickly at them then set the neat stack of wraps aside.

"Are they all cotton?"

"Yes."

"I don't usually sew such light fabric but I have some home sewers that work for me sometimes; they may be able to do the work," he said as he lit a cigarette.

"I'd suggest that you use a clear thread to close the opening. It wouldn't show and we wouldn't have to change threads. It would be cheaper for you."

"That sounds good," I said naively. *If I had only known.*

He dismissed me, but as I stood and reached to take my samples back, he put his hand on them.

"You don't mind if I keep these do you?"

"Oh, no that's fine." I said, wondering way he needed more instruction on how to sew two pieces of fabric together and why he needed to keep all of my samples.

I left with this bad feeling in my gut like I'd just been taken.

When I finally got my sewn wraps back there were some missing, and the quality of sewing was very poor. The closing stitch was indeed done in a clear thread; in fact it was fishing line! And to top it off they all smelled like cigarette smoke. I had to have the openings re-stitched, and all of the wraps, hundreds of them, had to be washed and ironed.

"Did you get your wraps back?" Roger asked me the day I picked them up.

"Yes,"

"You don't look too happy."

"I'm not," I said, wanting to cry. "I can't sell them this way."

"What? What's wrong with them?"

I proceeded to tell him what I'd discovered.

"Well take them back and make him do it right!"

"It's not that easy." I said. "To begin with I could have been to blame for some of the inconsistency because I did all the cutting."

"Yea, but you aren't to blame for the fishing line, the smoke and the missing inventory."

"No" I said, feeling like I'd really failed.

"It's too late in the season to redo all the wraps myself, and I can't afford to have them done again right."

"Why weren't you more careful?" he said

"Sweetie, this is all new to me. I'm going to make mistakes. It doesn't help for you to rub it in."

He looked at me, but the emotional support I was hoping for just wasn't there. I was in over my head, and we both knew it.

"I'm sorry." He said, softening a little.

"It's alright. I'm so busy with work, kids, and helping you with the ranch, I'm almost relieved that I don't have to try to do the test market this year anyway."

"Well you might as well just enjoy the holiday season then and pick up again next year" he said as he took my hand and pulled me to my feet. He put his arms around me.

"You know Simply Wrapped doesn't have to happen overnight."

"I know," I said. "But I'd settle for some point in my lifetime. It just seems like it is taking so long to bring this idea to life."

"Honey, look over there," he pointed to the gifts under the Christmas tree all wrapped in Simply Wrapped. "What do you call that? They are beautiful, sweetheart and you did it. This is your baby. Even if you do nothing else with Simply Wrapped, you've changed our family and how we give a gift."

"Thank you, I needed to hear that." I said snuggling up against his shoulder.

"Be patient with yourself," he said. "It will come."

TESTING THE MARKET

It wasn't until 1999 that I was able to do a small test market in our area to see how the idea would be received. My test market in Spokane consisted of in-home shows and word of mouth. People loved the concept but only a small percent felt the cost of a reusable fabric wrap outweighed the benefits. It was so much cheaper to buy disposable paper wrap. What most of them didn't know then was a lot of the paper wrap isn't even recyclable. Much of the paper will sit in landfills for a very, very long time before it ever begins to disintegrate.

"Are you okay?" Roger asked when I got home from doing my final show.

"Yes, just a little discouraged."

"What happened?"

"Well, they liked the idea a lot and a few of them purchased the kits, but most of them just couldn't get past the additional cost."

"It's not that much more than an expensive paper."

"I know, but they are comparing the prices to paper on sale at K-Mart."

"When's the last time you bought paper to wrap our gifts?" he asked, wanting to prove a point.

"I haven't bought paper to wrap gifts for family or even friends since 1994, five years ago."

"Did you tell them that?"

"No. I wanted to ask them when they would get tired of giving a gift surrounded by some trash, but I didn't."

"That's what it is though," Roger said.

"Yeah, well maybe someday people will see that our resources are not endless, that giving a gift, the whole gift, from the heart is more valuable than any disposable paper, and that traditions are the one thing that keeps us together when everything else is falling apart."

"Someday" Roger agreed as he handed me a glass of wine and raised his own.

"To your Dad, and to Simply Wrapped...someday."

It was clear that while Simply Wrapped was a great idea, the timing was very important and it was not quite right yet. People were just not ready to embrace the concept, and I had a lot more to learn about business and the textile industry in particular. Besides, we had a family to feed so my working was essential. For the following five years, as the holiday season approached, I'd brush off my Simply Wrapped dream. I'd purchase new prints for my family collection and sew the wraps myself. And in doing so, I'd work to make real another small part of the Simply Wrapped product line.

SANTA CLAUS THE BOX MAKER

Ever since the first years of Simply Wrapped I'd envisioned having a box that was specially designed to hold a family's collection of wraps and accessories. So after several years of Simply Wrapped being a part of our own family tradition and my storing our collection in paper boxes, I decided I needed to do the next thing to keep Simply Wrapped alive. I needed the Simply Wrapped Family custom-made Collection Box. I went looking for a master box maker, someone who loved making wooden boxes. I found him, and his name was Charlie, a.k.a. "Santa Claus."

Charlie was in his mid fifties, had shoulder length white hair, a bushy white beard that hung to his collar bones, and a round protruding stomach. Every year for the last several years, Charlie donned a costume and played Santa Claus in Manhattan. He was there the year after 9/11. He said he would never do it again; it was just too sad. The need in the eyes of the children was heart breaking. He then changed the subject to woodworking, which was clearly his passion. He told me about how his grandfather had taught him how to work with wood, and that he was the one who had given him the love of making boxes. He got very excited when I showed him Simply Wrapped and described the box I needed.

"I love this idea," he said. "I've got eight grand children and we are always giving them gifts. It would be so nice not to have to use paper."

I explained to him what I'd need in a box, and the general dimensions. I left the exact design of the box up to him; I wanted it to be a work of art, like a gift that is wrapped in Simply Wrapped. We agreed on a price and a delivery time.

"It's beautiful, Charlie," I said when we met a couple of weeks later. Charlie just smiled and relaxed into his chair.

He had created a unique box that held all of my family wraps and the accessories I used. Plus it was a size I was able to lift and easily store. It was a great piece of woodworking. He appeared happy, but something was bothering him.

"There's something I need to talk to you about," he said after I'd paid him for his work.

"Last week someone broke into my shop and stole all my tools."

"Oh, that's terrible, Charlie, I'm so sorry."

"I still have my grand father's hand tools and a table saw but it would take a long time to make the boxes the old fashioned way. I'd try to get a loan but we are not in a very good financial situation right now with me out of work and my wife not able to work."

I didn't know what to say. Santa needed a hand up and I didn't have a hand to give. "I'm sorry to hear that Charlie."

"I'll let you know if they recover my tools. And maybe we can continue from there. I'd really like to make the boxes for Simply Wrapped," he said as he got up to leave.

"If there is anyway we can make it happen, Charlie, we will." I said, knowing in the back of my mind that the funds my father left me were too limited to help him.

Christmas came again, and I pulled out the box Charlie had made for me, now full of my personal family collection of wraps carefully folded and layered inside. They were familiar prints; Hunter Gone Fishing for Papa, Star Gazers for Roger, Santa for Colby, and so on, each wrap chosen especially for the recipient.

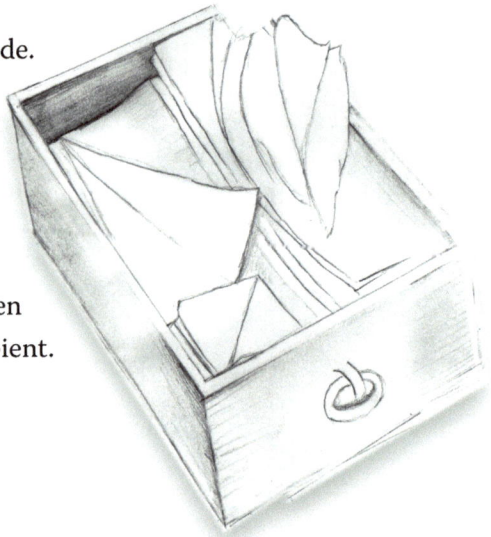

WOULD YOU PLEASE JUST GIVE UP!

Having the Simply Wrapped Family Collection Box helped me feel like at least I had not given up. Santa wasn't going to be able to make my boxes since he had not recovered the stolen tools, but before Dad died he taught my sister Susie how to make beautiful boxes and I knew one day she'd be able to help. It was 2004, ten years since I first conceived the idea but things still weren't lining up for me to take Simply Wrapped any further at that time. People were just not all that concerned about the environment and didn't get the importance of tradition and of giving a single gift from the heart versus a dozen gifts purchased out of a feeling of guilt or obligation. And I had some serious challenges with the costs of raw product and manufacturing. I'd learned over the years how to do all the manufacturing myself. I even had prints of my own designed, but the cost of doing things locally was just too high. I knew I needed to act like a big company and go overseas directly to the fabric manufacturers and to the sewers in order to be competitively priced.

I drew some sense of satisfaction knowing that our family had reduced the number of gifts to one or two per person and I hadn't bought paper wrapping for my family in over ten years. Simply Wrapped had become an integral part of our family holidays, birthdays, and any gift-giving occasion. We recognized the prints and it was good to see them again and again.

"Honey, you can't keep this up with Simply Wrapped. I just can't see how it's going to make any money and certainly not enough to support anyone let alone a family of four." Roger told me as he sat at my desk looking down at the beautiful box on the floor, filled with wraps.

I sat, quiet tears welling up in my eyes, as I thought of Dad and all that I'd done to this point. I didn't have an answer for him. He was right, Simply Wrapped was a failure; I was a failure.

"It's a great idea, honey." He said trying now to bolster my spirits, but it was too late. "We've just had too many losses over the last years for you to spend any more time and money on this idea. You need to go back to work, find a job in high-tech again, make some money."

Again he was right. Over the years since we had moved to Washington we had restored my husband's family ranch and built it up to working condition. But beef prices had dropped, his father and partner had died, my father was gone, three other members of our family had died and on top of it all, the forests on our ranch had burned up twice in two consecutive years, turning trees that were over 350 years old into a thousand torches. The value of our fourth generation ranch had plummeted.

It was a hard time, one that might have caused me to put my dreams of Simply Wrapped away for good, if it hadn't been for one rainy day and a moment of synchronicity.

I was looking out the window over our burned up ranch, remembering all those beautiful trees that were gone now, and I remember thinking,

I need to give up on this idea of bringing something useful into the world and get a "real" job.

I decided that instead of getting deeper into my depressed state, I would go out and try to find a book for a friend of mine who was feeling down herself. We both shared the love of reading, and a trip to the book store was a healthier thing for me to do than stand around pondering devastation. I made the forty-five minute drive into town becoming more and more convinced that this idea of Simply Wrapped needed to be put away for good.

I didn't have a particular book in mind for my friend, so when I arrived at the store I just scanned the shelves. I noticed on the top shelf facing out was a book titled "Work and the Human Spirit."

Now that's a book I could probably use. If it's time to give up on my entrepreneurial pursuits and get a job, it would be great if that job lifted my spirits.

I took the book down and flipped it open. The dedication read "To Boone."

The blood rushed from my head, I felt tingly all over. Boone is my maiden and middle name and the name I went by in college. I turned to the back of the book where the dedications were given in more detail and read:

"For Boone, for never giving up..." I sat down, book in hand, and stared at the words.

I've experienced synchronicity in my life before but not with such a specific relation to the current situation. It was both scary and exciting. And it didn't stop there.

Okay, since we're on a roll here, what am I not going to give up on?

I bought the book and another for my friend and I left the bookstore. On my way home I stopped at the library to pick up a couple of music CDs I'd ordered; I wanted to listen to some new music, something I'd never heard before...or so I thought.

I put one of the CDs on, poured myself a glass of wine and began making dinner. It was getting dark, the rain was still coming down and I was still confused about what to do about Simply Wrapped. I wasn't paying too much attention to the music still lost in thought when a song I recognized began to play.

"Tis a gift to be simple, Tis a gift to be free..."

That song...it's the one that gave me the idea for the name Simply Wrapped.

I poured my wine down the sink drain.

"Honey, you're right," I said to Roger over dinner that night. "I need to find work and I will, I promise, but I'm not going to give up on Simply Wrapped. Someday the world will want it, I just know it."

"If you say so, I just hope you find work soon because we can't make it on what I make at my part-time jobs," he said.

I looked for months for work locally and nationally, and then just before Christmas of 2004, one of the interviews led to a job offer.

"Dear, they've offered me a job," I told Roger when he came home from work that night.

"That's great! Where is it?"

"Boulder, Colorado"

"Boulder, Colorado? Will they let you work from home?"

"No, it's not that kind of job. I'll need to be there. It's a Senior Program Manager position."

"How much are they offering you?

"That's not settled for sure but it is in the six figures."

"Jeeze!"

"You could take time off. It would be good for you," I said hoping to encourage him to look at the bright side.

"We'd have to move."

"Yes"

"Do you know anything about Boulder?"

"No. One of my college classmates once said it was really beautiful there. It's a college town."

"Let's think about it over the weekend." I said.

"Sweetheart," Roger said as he put his arms around me. "I'm proud of you."

THE RIGHT TIME, THE RIGHT PLACE

The move to Boulder took place in stages with Roger, Colby and Justin coming in six months after Colby finished his senior year in high school, and Justin had returned from Europe were he had taken a temporary job through his college. We had decided even though both our sons were now graduated from high school, that we would move one more time together as a family.

I packed only what I thought I'd absolutely need for six months of apartment living with one exception, a collection of Simply Wrapped gift wrappings and the box that contained the draft of my business plan, marketing collateral, and anything else related to Simply Wrapped. There was only enough room in the car for myself and Colby, now eighteen, who was to be my escort on the trip.

"I've checked the car over and done all the maintenance," Roger said as he helped me load my things in the car.

"Thank you." I said knowing he would have made very sure that the car was road worthy.

"You take care of your mom, Colby." Roger hollered after Colby who was loading his small suitcase in the car.

"Call me from the road," he said looking down at me as we said our tearful goodbyes.

"I will. Don't worry. We'll be fine."

"I'll worry less when I know you've made it safely."

GOOD NEWS BAD NEWS

The job I took in Boulder turned out to be a wonderful but short lived experience. The bad news was that a year and a half later, I didn't have a job. The good news was Boulder, Colorado in 2006 turned out to be the place and the time for Simply Wrapped to emerge into the world.

With Roger's support and time on my hands I was able to focus completely on Simply Wrapped. I set up a Colorado corporation for Simply Wrapped, found new suppliers and manufacturers (all non-smokers!) and launched *Simply Wrapped* the company.

I purchased two suitcases to use in my new career as "traveling sales woman." One I filled with my basic wrapping kit which included the booklet I created in our half finished farm house and the other with props and sample wraps to use in demonstrations. Then I enlisted the help of my friend Deb who agreed to assist me with the numerous demonstration shows I'd lined up. The fall of 2006 was a very busy season. The response was promising. On average eight out of ten people to whom I presented Simply Wrapped purchased from my small product line. People were finally ready for *Simply Wrapped, The Gift on the Outside* [*].

FEEDBACK FROM CUSTOMERS

One of my favorite customers, an inventor herself, told me, "I've decided that my gifts either go wrapped in Simply Wrapped, or not wrapped at all." She is the kind of person who only gives a few gifts a year and wants the gifts to mean something when she does.

Another customer wrapped a gift that was sent to Israel to a man and his family. She received a lengthy letter back thanking her for the gift but especially for the wrap. It turns out that the man was a Rabbi and the wrap became an important part of their Hanukah ceremonies. One customer told me about a gift, a child's book about going on a safari, that she had wrapped for the young child. The print for that particular wrap contains whimsical images of penguins. When the boy was looking at his book (the gift) he became upset.

"Where are the penguins?" he asked as he searched the book over. *The penguins?* my friend thought, and then she remembered the wrap and, unfolding it, handed it to the child,

"Here they are," she said. And there they were. The Gift on the Outside.

Simply Wrapped gifts went that year to California, Massachusetts, Oregon, Washington, Idaho, Florida, New York, Israel, various places in Colorado and a number other places I couldn't track. My customers were overwhelmingly pleased with Simply Wrapped with one exception.

They wanted and needed a book on how to wrap, to help them over the learning curve.

THE FIRST HAPPY ENDING

As I finish writing this book I'm sitting in my home office, evidence of my entrepreneurial journey with Simply Wrapped on the walls, my desk, and in the lighted walnut cabinet where I display the various styles of wrapping. Several versions of the basic wrapping kit are neatly stacked on the second shelf of the cabinet. The light shines down and catches the gold in one of the ornate prints that are still so popular with my customers.

A revised version of the first instruction booklet I made using a makeshift light table in the living room of our unfinished old farm house sits on my desk. The first and second drafts of the cover of this book are pinned to a cork board on the wall to my right. I look around at all of this evidence, proof that gifts are meant to be treasured. Proof that my dad was right. Proof that no matter what, I never gave up.

So I want you to consider this book my gift to you. The remainder of the book contains directions for the twelve basic wraps that I teach people how to do. They really are simple. And once you master those, let your imagination lead the way. The possibilities are endless.

Have fun, be creative, and I hope you develop your own traditions of giving with Simply Wrapped! Oh, and be sure to send me your Simply Wrapped stories to stories@simplywrappedgifts.com. That's part of my tradition, and I hope you think it's worth continuing.

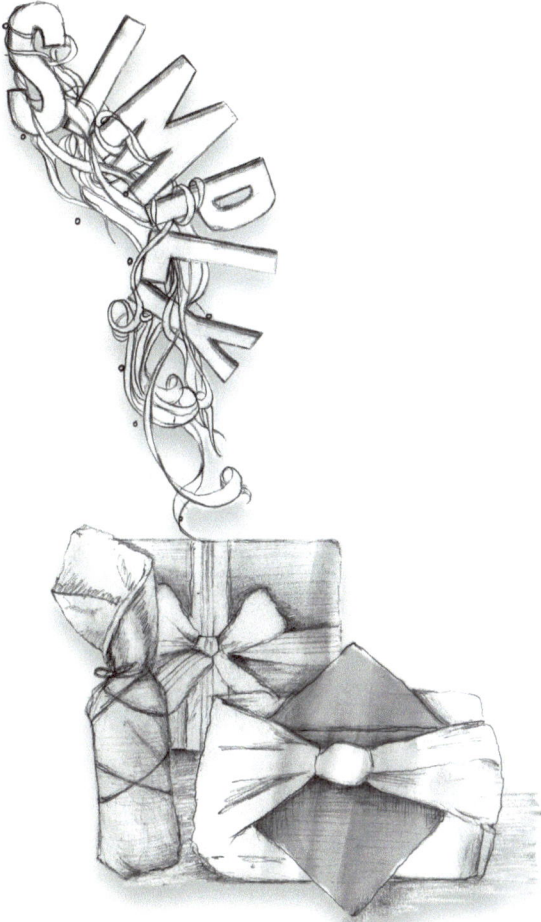

Wrapping Styles

NOW IT'S TIME TO WRAP your gift or gifts. They are sitting in front of you lined up. You are feeling good about having found the right presents for each individual, but you may also be feeling tired, rushed, stressed about all that you have to do (though you'd not admit it) and wondering how you are going to get these gifts wrapped in anything less than two hours. Here's a secret about Simply Wrapped. Not only is it environmentally friendly, it doesn't take as long as paper wrapping—and your presents look just as good or even better! So let me give you a few pointers to help you get started as you approach the task of wrapping in Simply Wrapped.

1 **WORK AREA**—have a large, cleared flat surface to work on, your dining room table for example.

2 **GIFTS AND SUPPLIES**—have your gifts, wraps, and accessories (rings, ribbons, etc.) handy as well as scissors if you intend to use ribbon that will need to be cut to size.

3 INSTRUCTIONS—have the Simply Wrapped book with instructions available if this is your fist time wrapping in Simply Wrapped.

4 REMEMBER—you are wrapping in fabric. It is not going to behave like paper with permanent creases and that crumpling sound. If you don't get the look you want you can do it again as many times as you like.

5 ATTITUDE—have the person in mind when you wrap. Being able to give a gift to someone you care about is an act of love. When I wrap, I get excited about this gift I'm giving to my loved one. (I have also found that when I approach wrapping my gifts from a sense of obligation or guilt, I am likely not going to enjoy what I'm doing. When I find I'm not enjoying it, I just simply change my attitude!)

Take pleasure in the process, and may you never approach gift-giving in the same way again!

Three Point

SMALL RING
1" diameter

SMALL BOX
4" cube style

1

Lay wrap on flat surface
print side down. Place gift on
wrap diagonally as shown.

SMALL WRAP
18" square

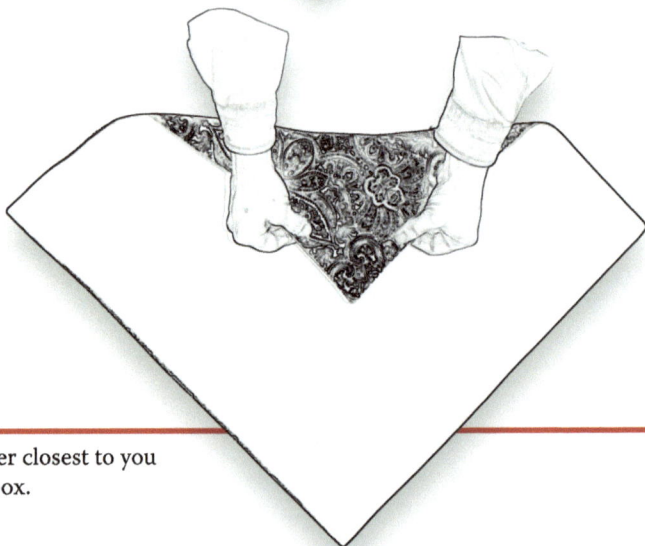

2

Fold corner closest to you
over the box.

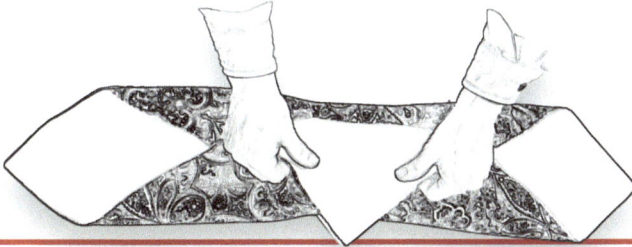

3

Bring opposite corner over the
gift and fold back exposing the
solid colored side of wrap.

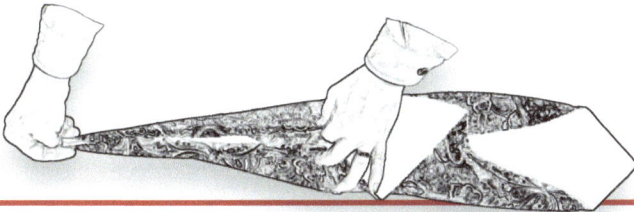

4

Holding edges with one hand,
pull the fabric to a point
with the other hand.

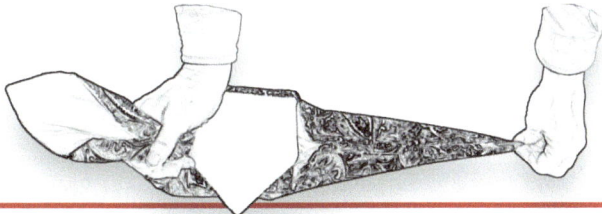

5

Bring this point to top of gift
and hold, then with free hand
gather the second point.

6

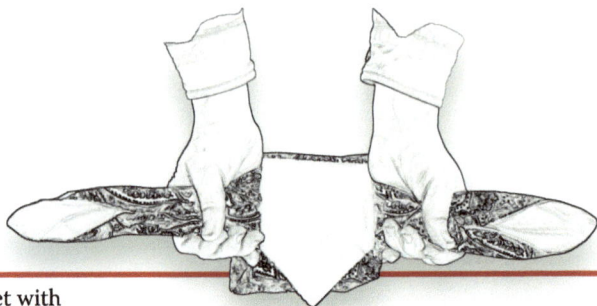

Fold up to meet with
the first point.

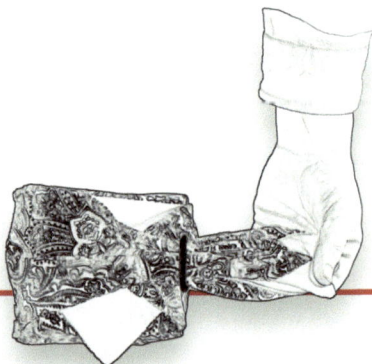

7

Pull both points through
the ring.

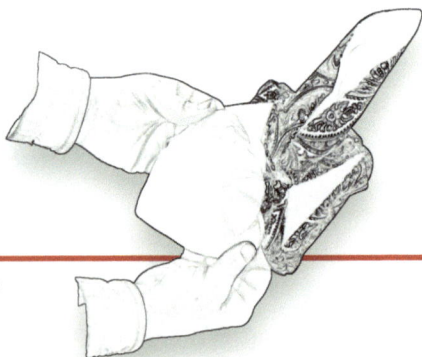

8

Invert points to show inside
solid color fabric for finish.

Three Point Wrap

Book Pocket

ANY BOOK
Wrap size varies
depending on
size of book
or box.

1

Lay wrap on a flat surface,
solid colored side up, with
your book (or boxed gift)
in the center.

MEDIUM WRAP
20 to 22" square

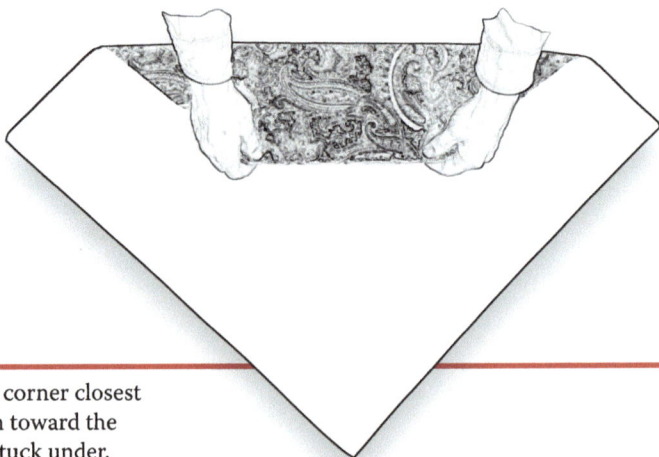

2

Fold the corner closest
to you in toward the
gift and tuck under.

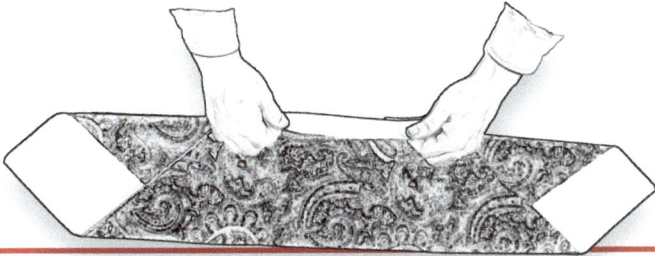

3

Roll the opposite corner
over the gift and roll back
to the center.

4

You're going for the
look of a ribbon.

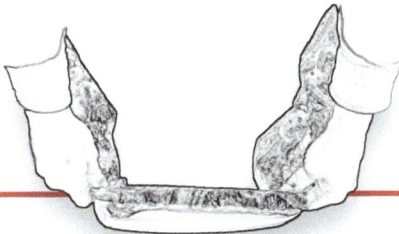

5

Holding tight to the ends,
carefully turn your gift over so
the solid stripe is on the underside.

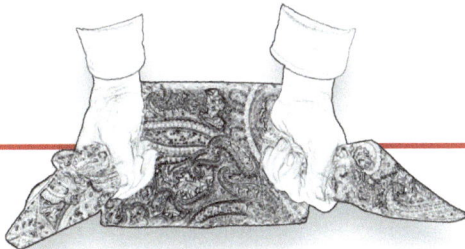

6

Take hold of both ends of
the wrap close to the gift.

7

Tie ends into a
square knot.

8

Arrange the ends to
create a bow.

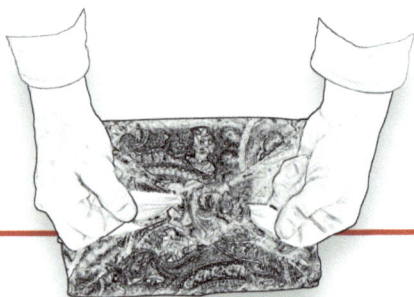

9

Finish with a
personalized card.

Book Pocket Wrap

Ribbon Bow

WRAP STYLE 3

RIBBON
Use any width
or color

MEDIUM BOX
Box size may vary

MEDIUM WRAP
20 to 22″ square

1

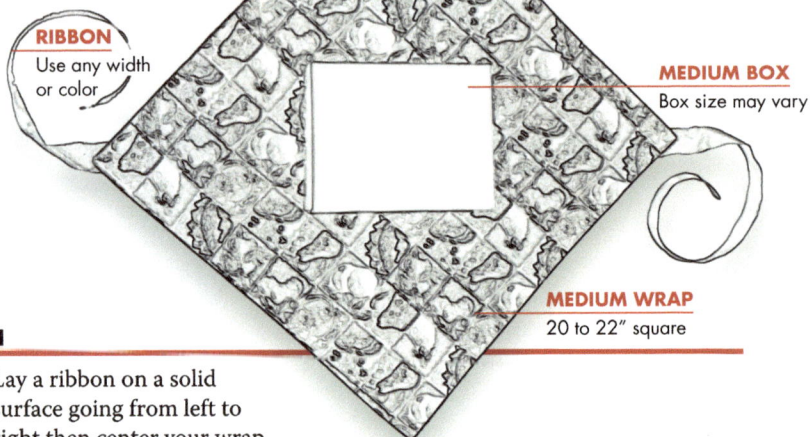

Lay a ribbon on a solid
surface going from left to
right then center your wrap
diagonally on top of it,
solid colored side down.
Place the gift in the center.

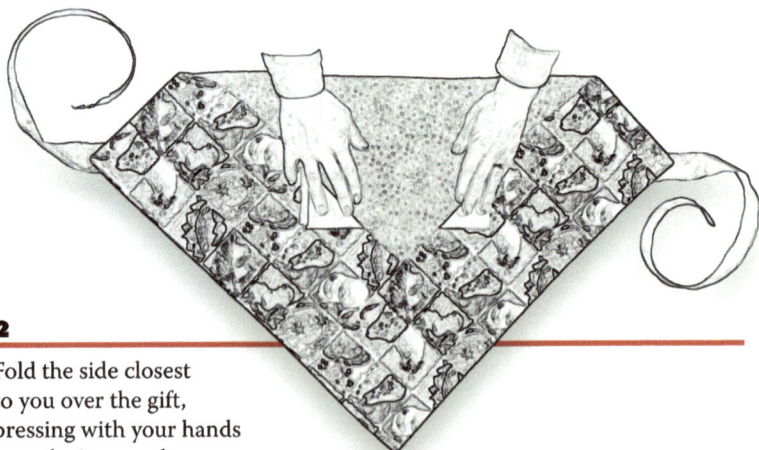

2

Fold the side closest
to you over the gift,
pressing with your hands
to make it smooth.

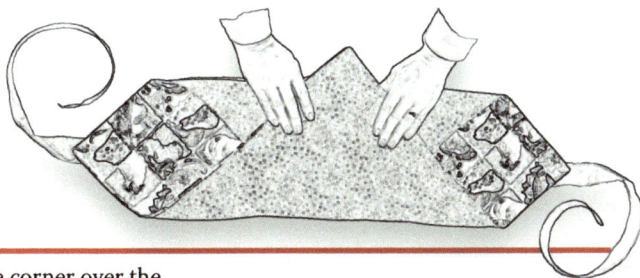

3

Bring opposite corner over the
gift and tuck the hanging corner
under to conceal the pattern
side of wrap.

4

Fold both ends to form
points much like you do
with paper.

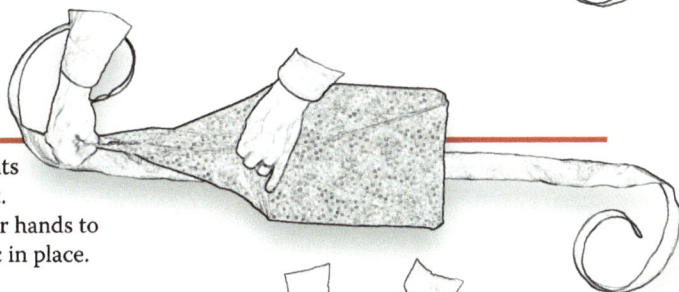

5

Fold both points
in over the gift.
Press with your hands to
keep the fabric in place.

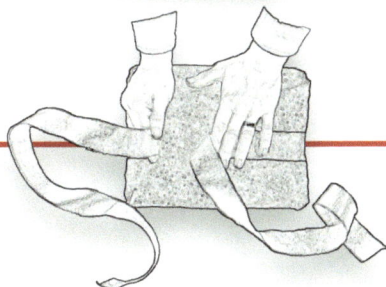

6

Take both ends of the ribbon
and pull them together in
the center of the gift.

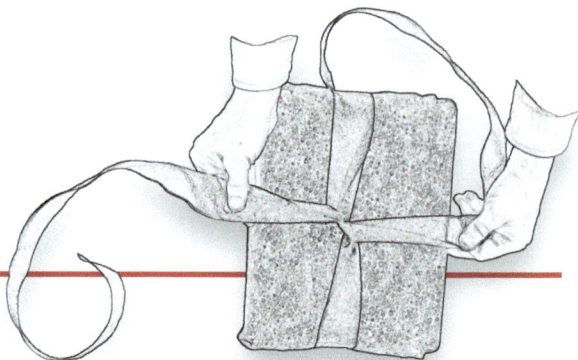

7

Wrap the ribbon
in your right hand
around the one in
your left.

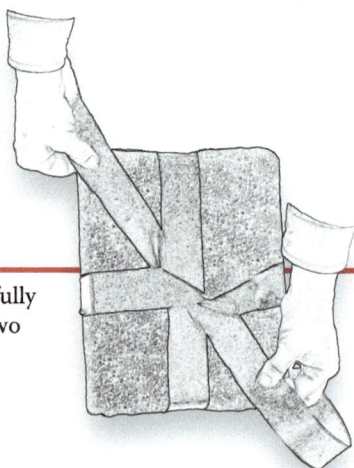

8

Still holding the ribbon, carefully
turn the gift over, bring the two
ends together again.

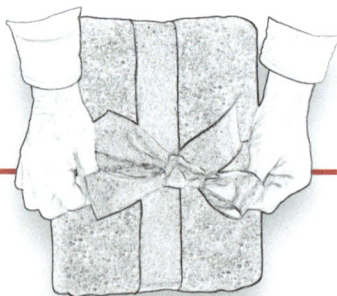

9

Tie a bow.

Ribbon Bow Wrap

Simple Knot

WRAP STYLE 4

MEDIUM BOX
Box size may vary

1

Lay wrap solid side
down diagonally on
large flat surface.
Place boxed gift in
the center of wrap
at the diagonal.

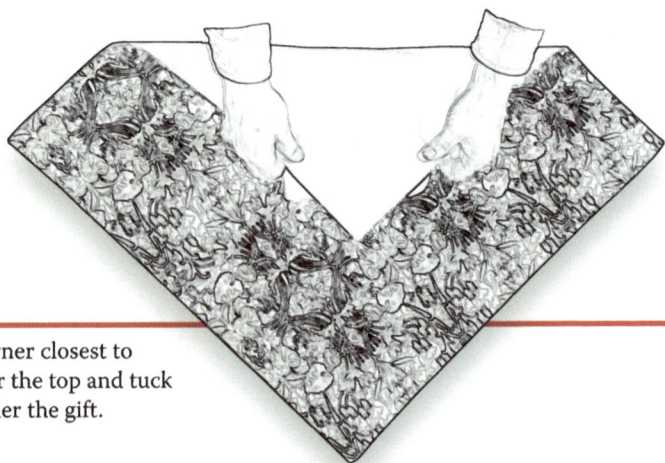

MEDIUM WRAP
20 to 22″ square

2

Fold corner closest to
you over the top and tuck
end under the gift.

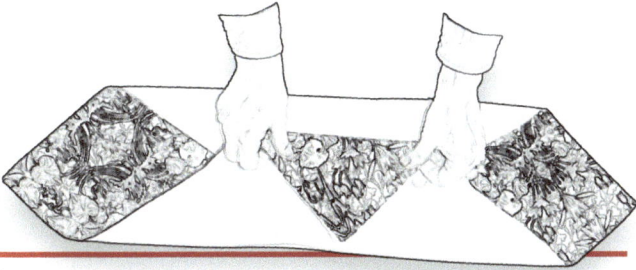

3

Bring opposite corner over
the gift and fold back exposing
print side of fabric in a point.

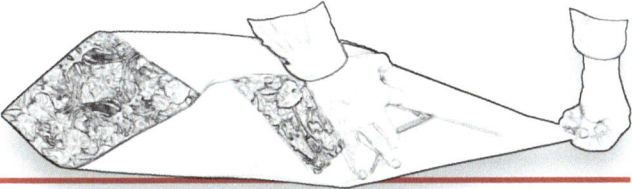

4

Grasping the point of fabric
to the right bring up and to
the center of the gift.

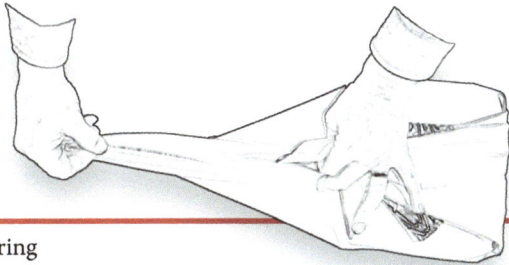

5

With other hand bring
the remaining point to
the top of gift.

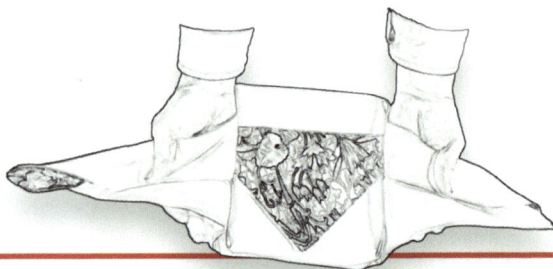

6

Take hold of **both ends of** the wrap close to **the gift.**

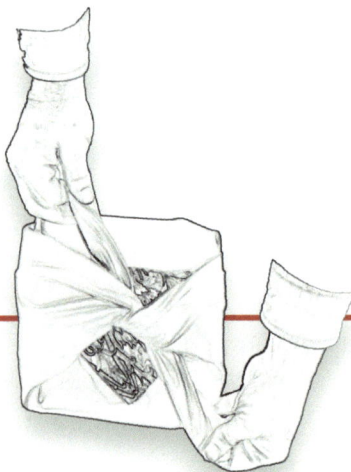

7

Tie a square knot in the center.

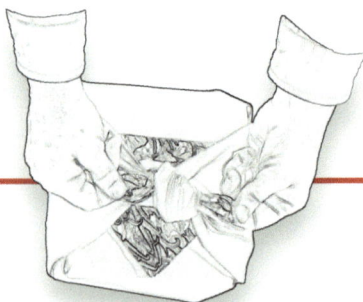

8

Arrange the ends to create a bow.

Simple Knot Wrap

Ring Tuck

SMALL BOX
Jewelry or broch

SMALL RING
1" diameter

SMALL WRAP
18" square

1

Lay wrap solid
side down on
flat surface
Place gift approximately
four inches from the edge
of the wrap.

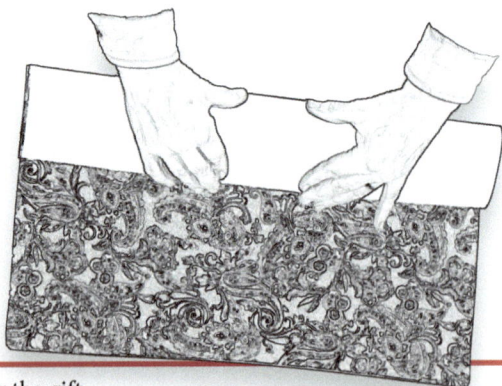

2

Fold edge of wrap over the gift.
Roll gift tightly in fabric until
about 6 in are left.

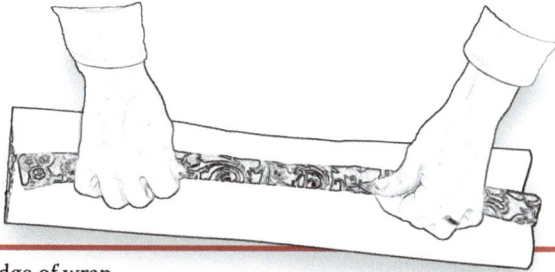

3

Bring opposite edge of wrap
over the gift and fold back
to expose print creating
a ribbon look.

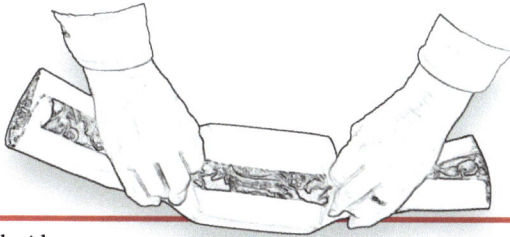

4

Pinch fabric on both sides
of gift. Flip gift over.

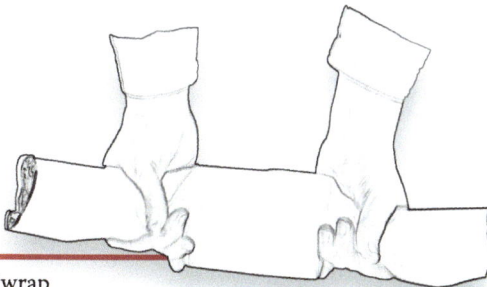

5

Grasp both ends of wrap
and bring up to top of gift.

6

Fold up to meet with
the first point. Pull
through the ring.

7

Flare fabric out to
expose print side.

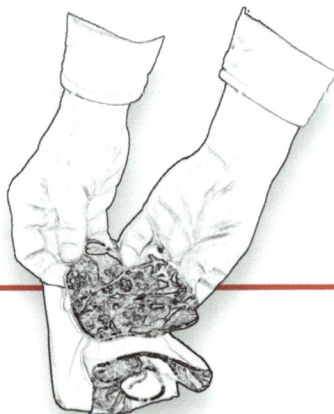

8

Create a blossom look.

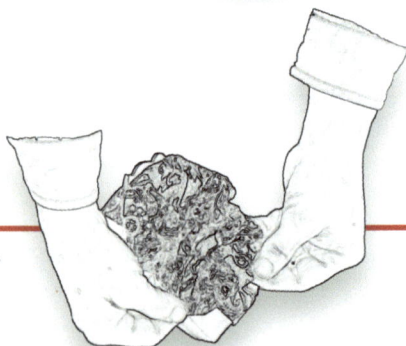

Ring Tuck Wrap

Two Point Knot

MEDIUM BOX
As box size varies
so does wrap size.

1

Lay wrap on flat surface
print side down with gift
centered toward bottom
of wrap.

MEDIUM WRAP
20" to 22" square

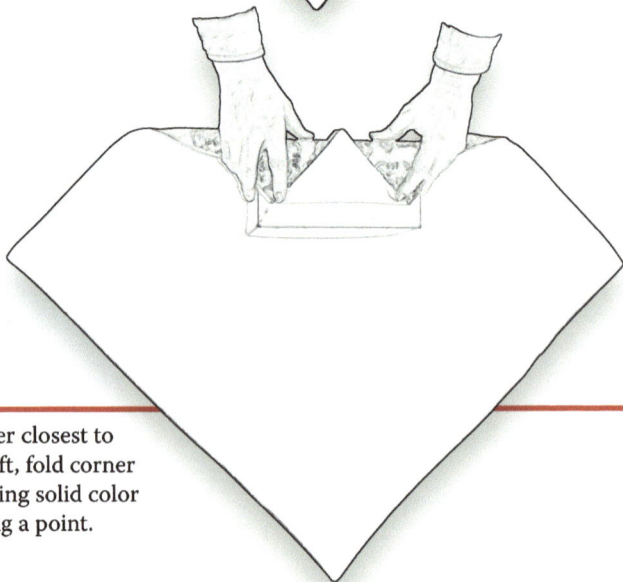

2

Bring corner closest to
you over gift, fold corner
back exposing solid color
and creating a point.

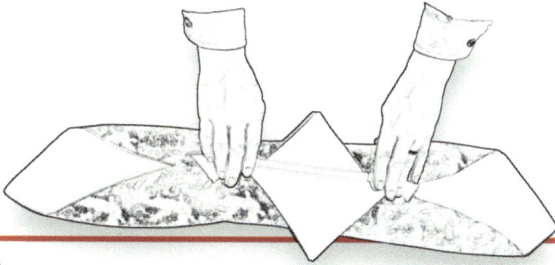

3

Do the same with
the opposite corner.

4

Pinch edges of wrap closest
to gift together with one hand
and create a point by pulling
opposite corner out away
from the gift.

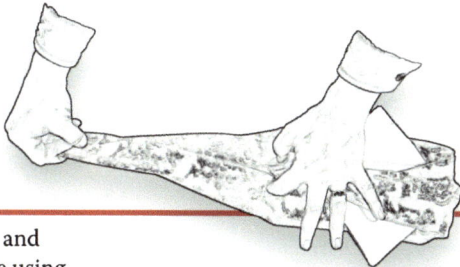

5

Bring point to top of gift and
hold with one hand while using
the other to bring the other
point to the top of the gift.

6

Take hold of both ends of
the wrap close to the gift.

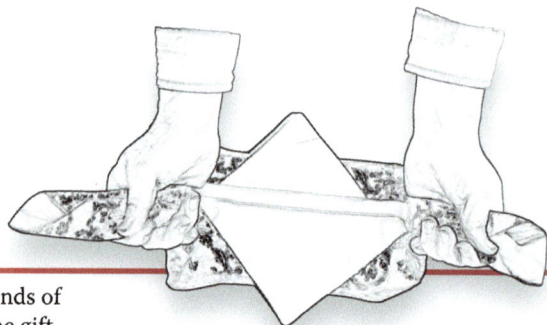

7

Tie a square knot
in the center.

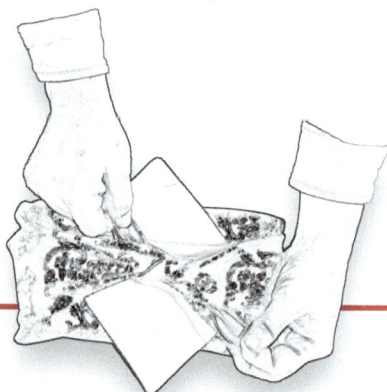

8

Arrange the ends to
create a bow.

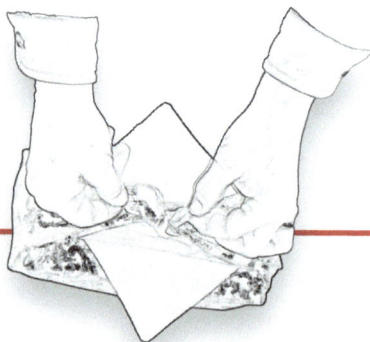

Two Point Knot Wrap

Clothing Roll

CLOTHING
Simply fold any
article of clothing.
Use appropriate
wrap size.

RIBBON
Use any width
or color

1

Lay wrap diagonally
on flat surface, print
side down. Place folded
clothing item on wrap.

MEDIUM WRAP
20 to 22" square

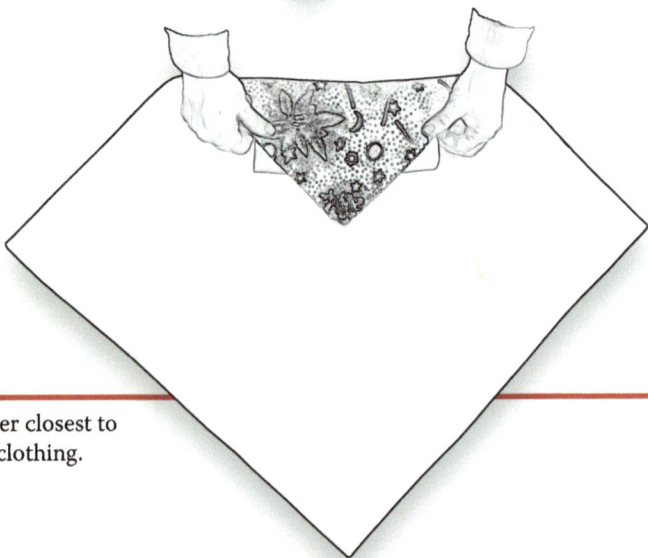

2

Fold corner closest to
you over clothing.

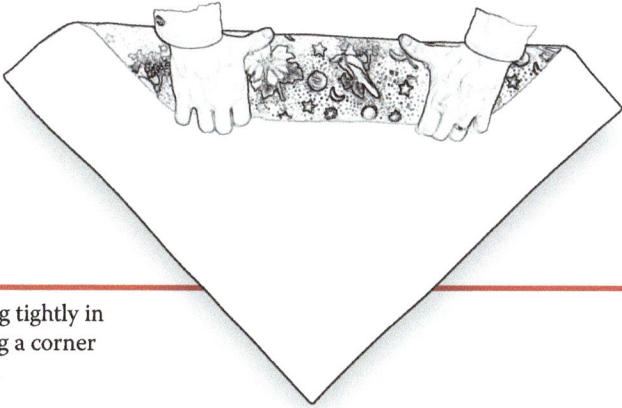

3

Roll clothing tightly in
wrap leaving a corner
of the wrap.

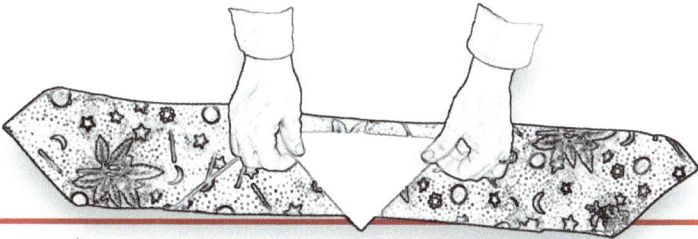

4

Bring opposite corner over
gift and fold back exposing
the solid side of wrap and
creating a point.

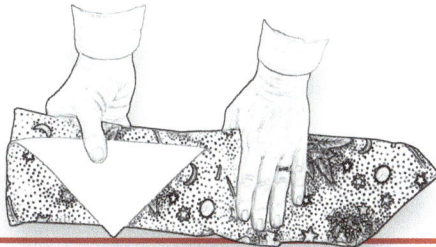

5

Gather ends close to clothing
and fold both under the gift.

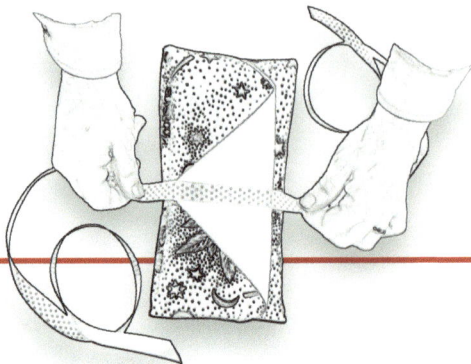

6

Start with ribbon on
the side with exposed
solid corner.

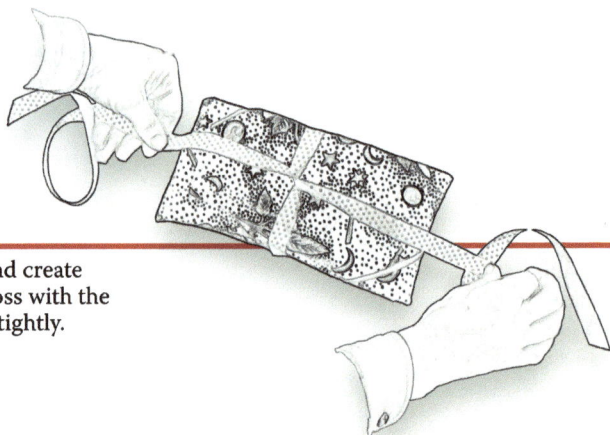

7

Turn over and create
a tension cross with the
ribbon held tightly.

8

Flip back over and finish
with simple ribbon bow.

Clothing Roll Wrap

Full Bloom

MEDIUM RING
1.5" to 2" diameter.
Try different ring
sizes to get a snug
fit against your gift.

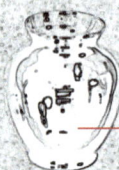

VASE
Any irregularly-
shaped item works
well with this style.

1

Lay your wrap on a
flat surface, solid color
side up, with one corner
pointing at you. Place
your gift in the center.

MEDIUM WRAP
20 to 22" square

2

Lift the corner closest
to you and the one opposite
together up over the gift.

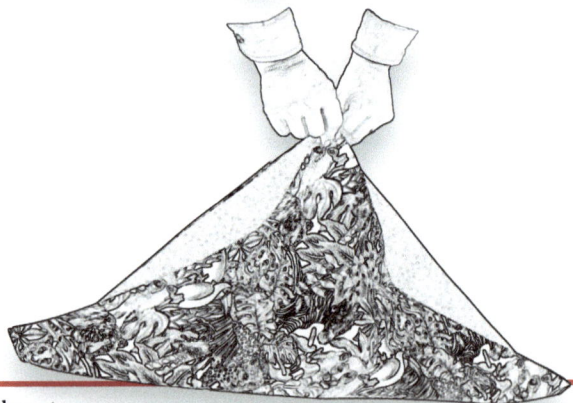

3

Lift the remaining two
corners together with
the first two.

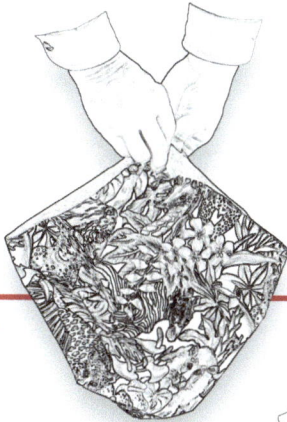

4

Place the medium ring over the
four ends and pull the wrap through.
Push the ring down until it is snug
against your gift.

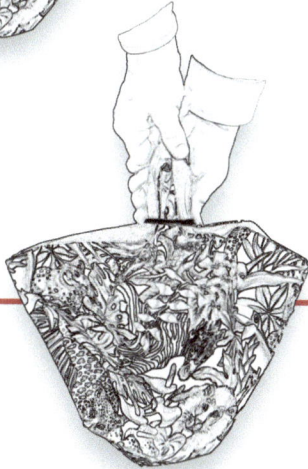

5

Stand your gift upright
and center the ring.

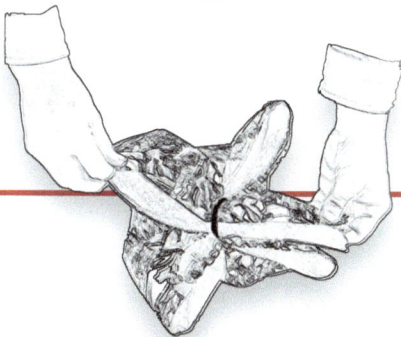

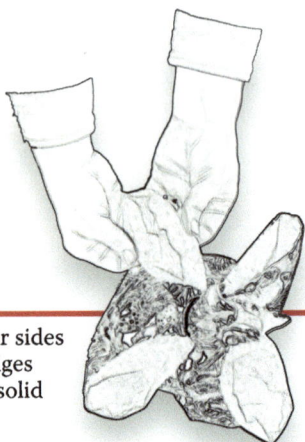

6

Pull each of the four sides
out and turn the edges
over to expose the solid
color of the wrap.

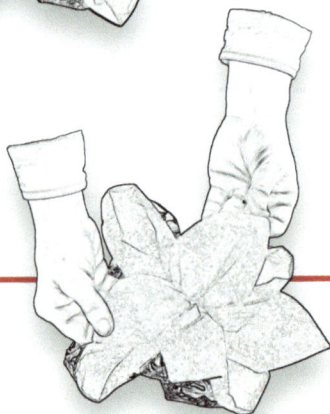

7

The corners that were threaded
through the ring can be folded
back for additional accent.

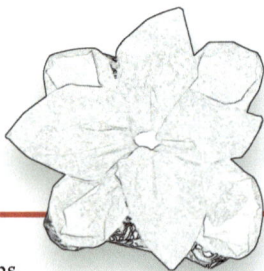

8

Two different
finishing options.

Full Bloom Wrap

Point Pull

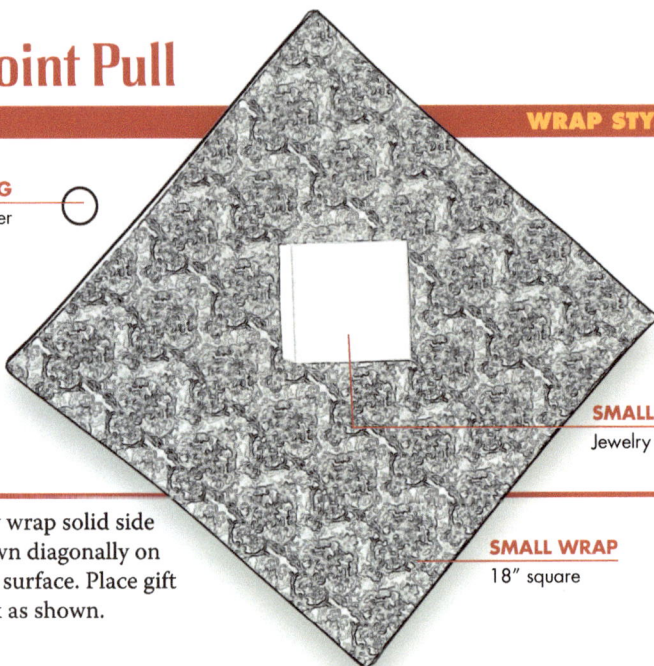

SMALL RING
1″ diameter

SMALL BOX
Jewelry style

SMALL WRAP
18″ square

1

Lay wrap solid side down diagonally on flat surface. Place gift box as shown.

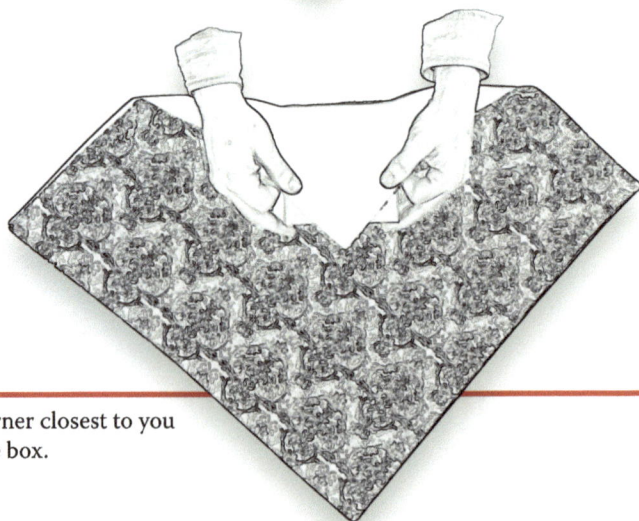

2

Fold corner closest to you over the box.

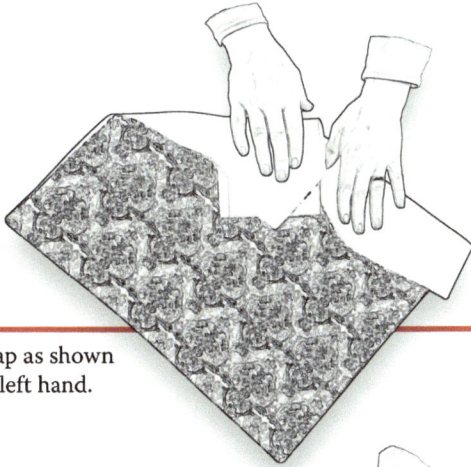

3

Fold corner of wrap as shown pressing out with left hand.

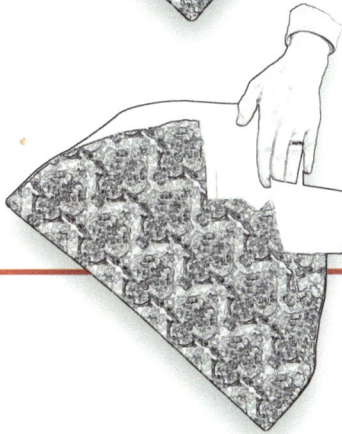

4

Bring this corner to top of gift and hold.

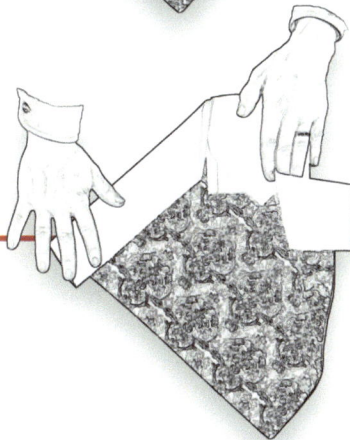

5

Fold opposite edge in the same way then bring this edge up to top of gift with other.

6

Hold both edges together at top of gift with one hand. With free hand pull final corner of wrap out to create a point.

(Note: Make sure you gather the wrap toward the edge of the box farthest away from you. This is what allows one point to be longer than the others.)

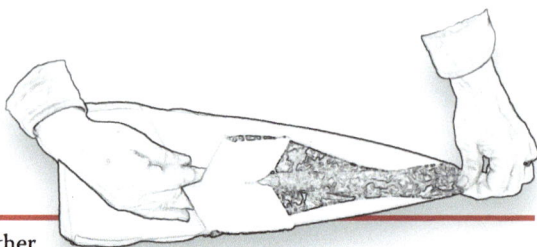

7

Pull all three corners through the ring.

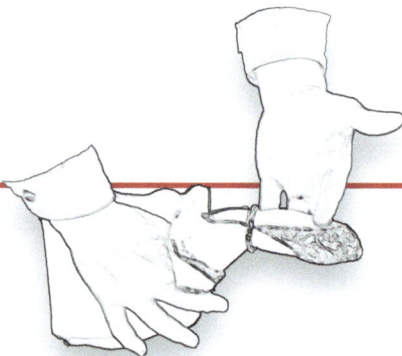

8

Fold two shorter corners out exposing the print. Pull the long point up to create a peak.

Point Pull Wrap

Jelly Roll

SMALL JAR
As jar size varies
so does the wrap size.

SMALL RING
1" diameter

SMALL WRAP
18" square

1

Lay wrap print side
down diagonally on
flat surface. Place gift
jar as shown.

2

Begin rolling the jar in
fabric away from you to
approximately the mid-
point of the wrap.

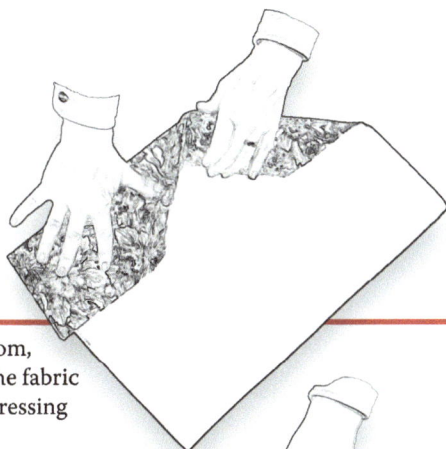

3

To create a flat bottom, fold one corner of the fabric in toward the gift, pressing out with hand.

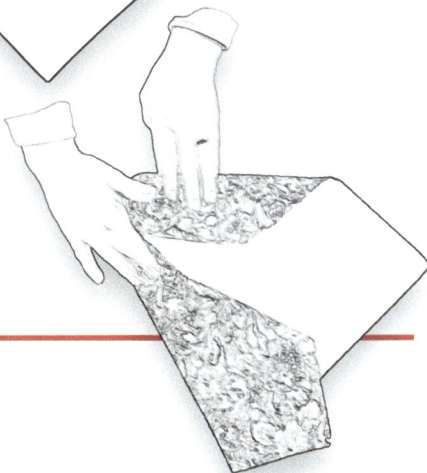

4

Fold the same corner again in the same way and then a third time. You should clearly see a stable base forming around the jar.

(Note: It is important to create a flat bottom so the git will stand up.)

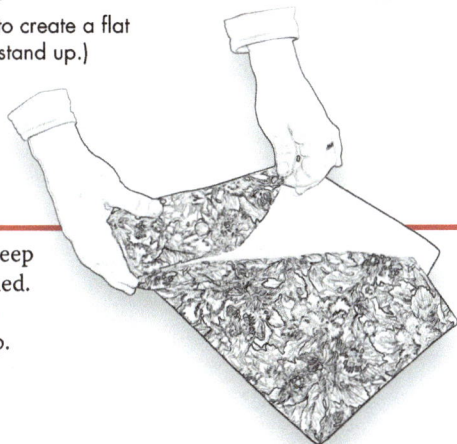

5

As you roll the jar, keep the fabric straightened. Doing this will help the corners stand up.

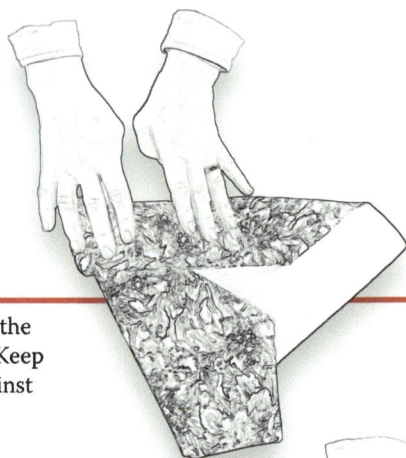

6

Roll the jar across the remaining fabric. Keep the wrap snug against the side of the jar.

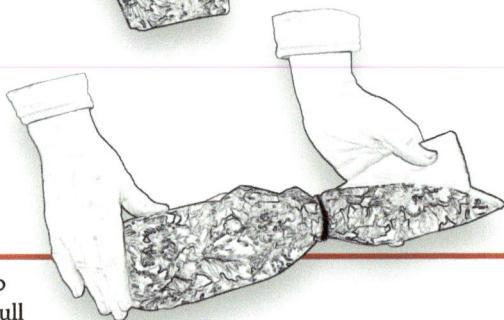

7

Holding the gift so wrap remains snug, lift and pull ring over the fabric points. Push the ring down tight against the gift.

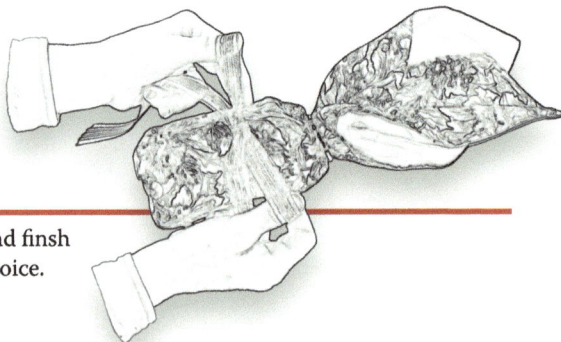

8

Flair the fabric points and finsh with a ribbon of your choice.

Jelly Roll Wrap

Single Bottle

RIBBON
Use any width
or color

WINE BOTTLE
Bottle sizes and
shapes may vary.

1

Lay wrap print
side down diagonally
on flat surface. Place
bottle as shown.

MEDIUM WRAP
20 to 22" square

2

Begin rolling the bottle
in fabric away from you
to approximately the
mid-point of the wrap.

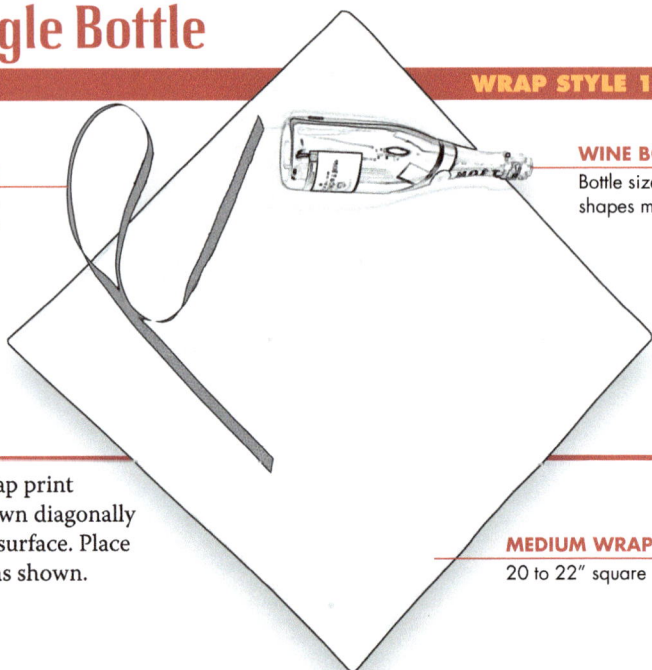

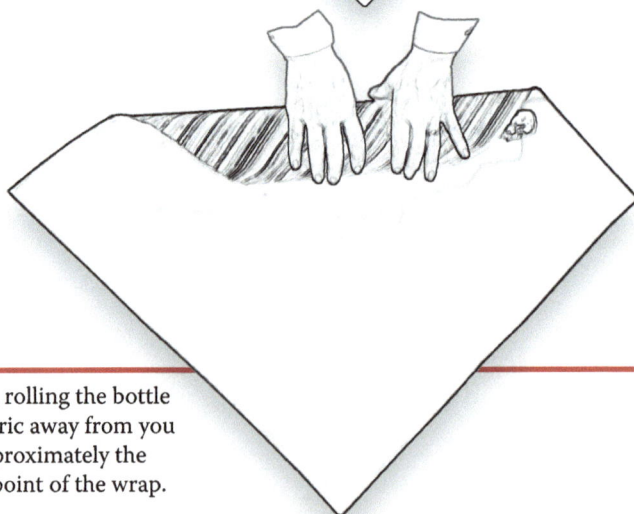

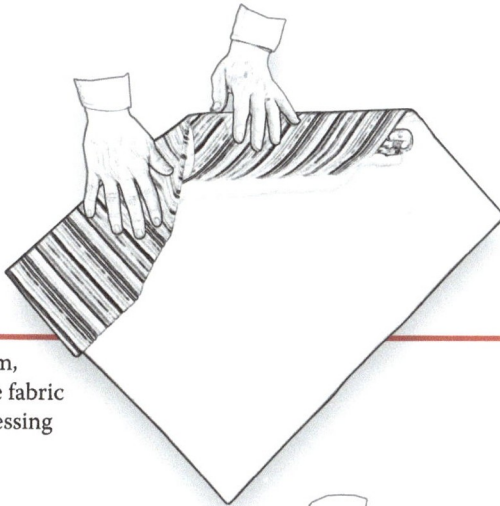

3

To create a flat bottom,
fold one corner of the fabric
in toward the gift, pressing
out with hand.

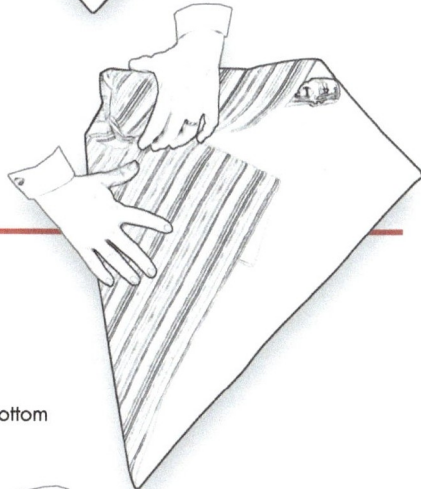

4

Fold the same corner again
in the same way and then
a third time. You should
clearly see a stable base
forming around the bottle.

(Note: It is important to create a flat bottom
so the git will stand up.)

5

Roll the bottle across the
remaining fabric. Keep
the wrap snug against
the side of the bottle.

6

As you roll, keep the fabric straightened. Doing this will help the corners stand up.

7

To secure fabric in place, wind ribbon around the gift starting at the bottom and criss-crossing toward the top of the bottle.

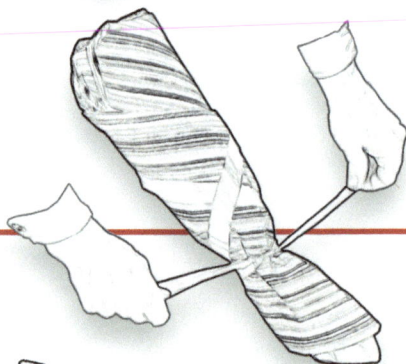

8

Finish the ribbon with a bow. For add accent, turn the edges of the wrap along the sides to expose the solid color.

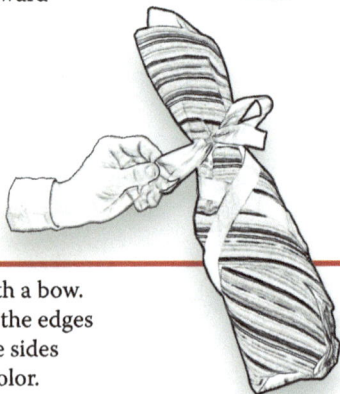

Single Bottle Wrap

Double Bottle

WINE BOTTLES
Bottle sizes and
shapes may vary.
The bottles shown are
petite (approx 6 oz).
Regualr wine bottles
require a large
wrap size.

1

Spread wrap on a flat surface.
Place two bottles on wrap as
illustrated with approximately
3 inches between the bottoms. For
standard wine bottles allow 4 inches
between the bottoms.

MEDIUM WRAP
20 to 22" square

2

Begin rolling the bottles in
fabric away from you.

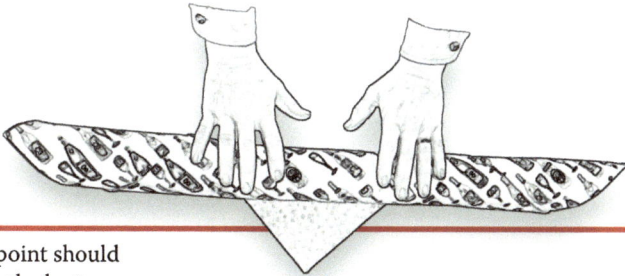

3

The fabric point should be between the bottoms of the bottles.

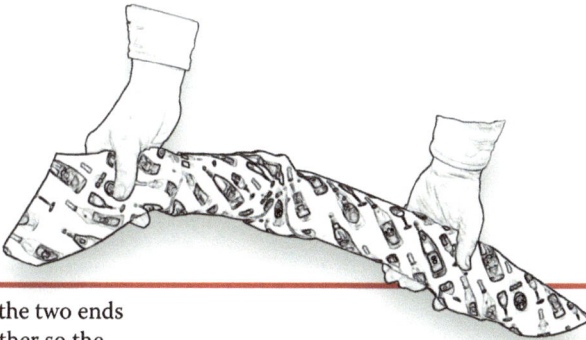

4

Take hold of the two ends and pull together so the bottles are standing up.

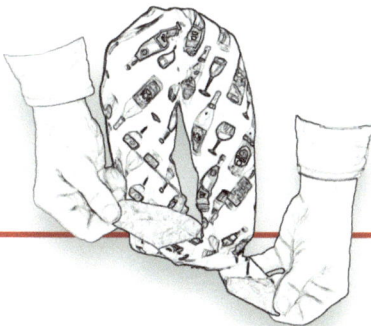

5

Now tie the ends together in a square knot.

6

Finish off the square knot.

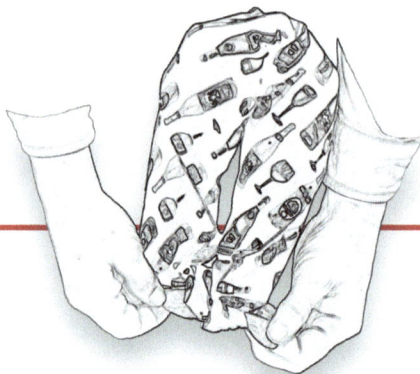

7

For added accent, turn the fabric to expose the opposite color fabric.

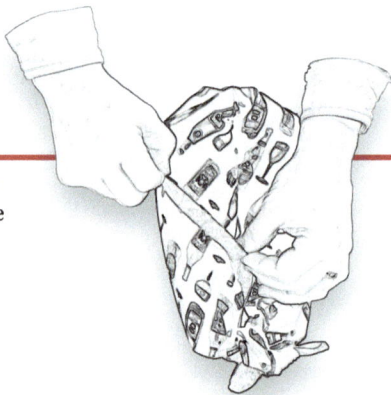

Double Bottle Wrap

The possibilities
are endless!

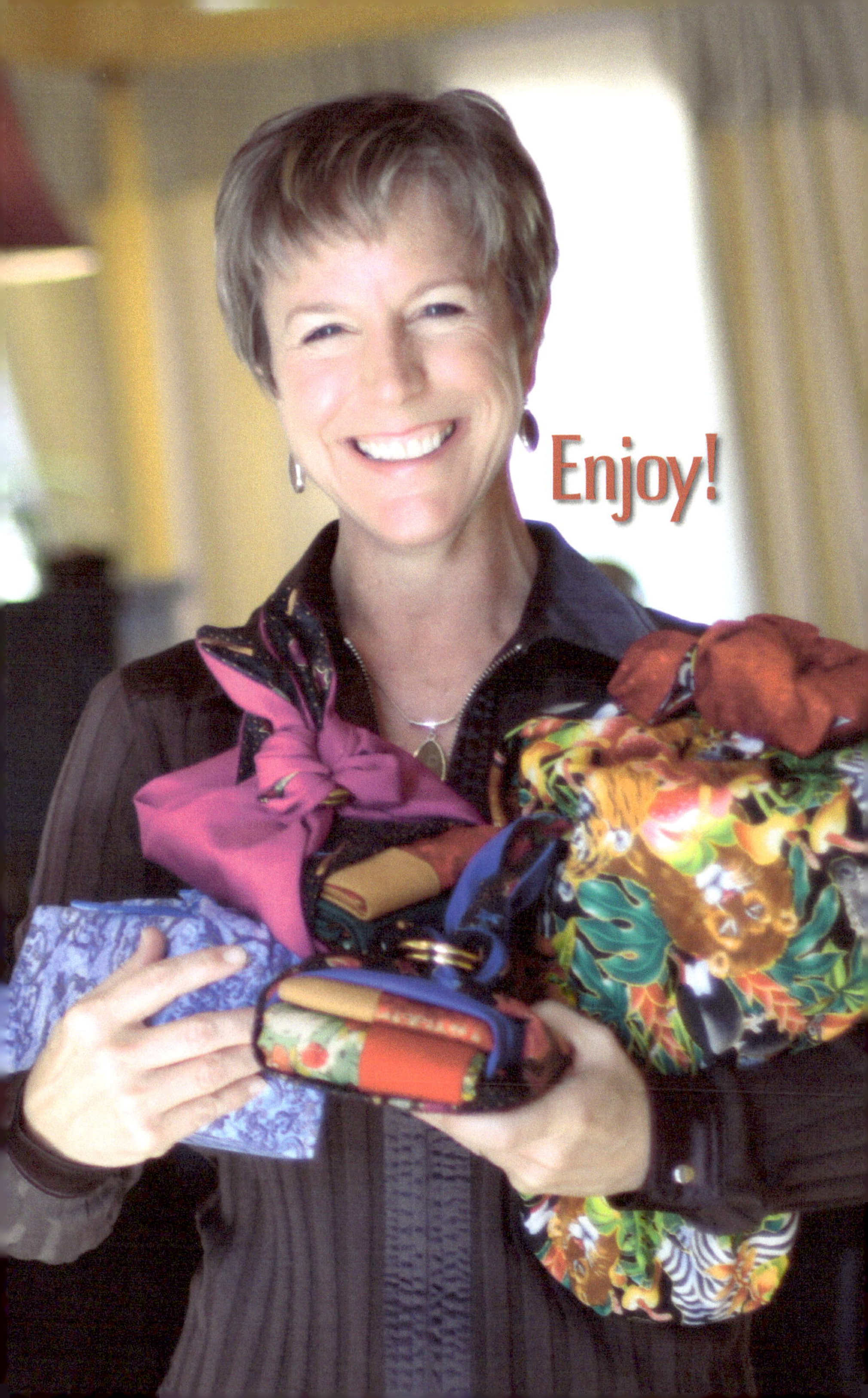
Enjoy!